THE
Archive Photographs
SERIES

BALBY
AND
HEXTHORPE

Houses under construction near the Shadyside/Laughton Road junction Hexthorpe, during July 1905, provide a backdrop for horse-drawn wagonettes conveying people to a picnic at Edlington.

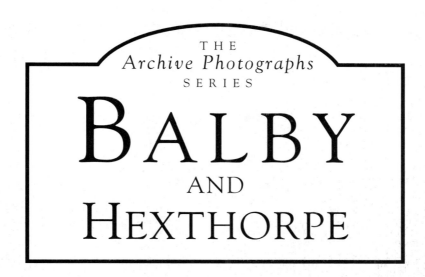

THE
Archive Photographs
SERIES

BALBY
AND
HEXTHORPE

Compiled by
Peter Tuffrey

CHALFORD

First published 1996
Copyright © Peter Tuffrey, 1996

The Chalford Publishing Company
St Mary's Mill, Chalford,
Stroud, Gloucestershire, GL6 8NX

ISBN 0 7524 0633 7

Typesetting and origination by
The Chalford Publishing Company
Printed in Great Britain by
Redwood Books, Trowbridge

A horse-and-trap pictured in front of the Balby tram terminus shelter at the High Road/Oswin Avenue junction. The shelter had to be locked at certain times to restrict vandalism and was eventually removed.

Contents

For Oscar Nelson

Introduction

Most of the Balby and Hexthorpe photographs included in this publication extend back over the last hundred years so, perhaps, it is worthwhile just to outline some of the main events from this period.

For much of their existence, Hexthorpe and Balby have been linked together. In 1831 Balby-with-Hexthorpe, as it was known, was described as: 'two pleasant villages forming a township of 420 inhabitants'. Hexthorpe and Balby were then a Rural District of Doncaster. In 1861, 1,058 people lived in Balby-with-Hexthorpe, the population expansion coinciding with Doncaster's development as a railway town, the Plant Works being opened in 1853. Also, around this time, two ecclesiastical parishes were formed: St John's, set up in 1846, had a population of 922 by 1871. St James' consecrated in 1858, was close to the town centre, and mainly used by GNR workers.

St Jude's church Hexthorpe, was erected in 1894 at a cost of £5,000 by the late Lord Grimethorpe and Miss Beckett-Dennison. St John's church, at Balby, was built in 1847. Also established were Wesleyan and Primitive Methodist chapels. The Doncaster Union Workhouse was built in Hexthorpe in 1840, which in turn was replaced by the Springwell Lane Workhouse and Hospital Balby, opening in 1900.

To cope with the influx of workers, many acres of land in Hexthorpe and Balby including nurseries and fields were gradually taken over for housing and commercial development. Some of Hexthorpe's streets were named after prominent townsmen like W. Sheardown, H. Senior, W. Shirley, Captain Ramsden and Beckett Denison. Amongst the companies establishing themselves in Hexthorpe were the Lincoln Wagon & Engine Works, T. Burnett's Hexthorpe Railway Wagon Works, and Woodhouse & Co's brass works.

The Plant Works' expansion at the turn of the century, including the erection of the Crimpsall Locomotive Repair Shop, Tender Shop and Paint Shop, extended railway activity along Hexthorpe's northern periphery.

In 1904, Fred Burchall and Frank Pegler moved from Union Street, in Doncaster to establish new brass workshops at the bottom of Belmont Avenue, Balby, the business becoming known as Peglers'.

Both Hexthorpe and Balby were served by trams from 1902, later replaced by trolley buses in 1929 and 1931 respectively, lasting until the early 1960s, when they were superseded by motorbuses.

Hexthorpe Flatts was thrown open to the public on August Bank Holiday 1902. The Flatts became one of Doncaster's favourite parks. It was a popular holiday centre for local families, particularly in the Edwardian period as it could be quickly reached and there was music, dancing, boating to enjoy, besides many recreational areas being available for children. The Flatts officially became a park in 1928, prior to that time, the term used to describe the location was pleasure or recreation area.

Amongst the other main events to occur in Hexthorpe during the present century are: the sharp rise then decline of industry in the area; the opening of the Plant Works recreation ground, covering over twelve acres at Eden Grove in 1914; house clearance and road alterations. When the Doncaster Borough was extended in 1914, Hexthorpe and Balby were also absorbed.

During the 1930s, Fisher's Park, Balby was transferred from private to public ownership, but it was not used to build houses. Instead, it was retained as a public open space. Sandford Road's construction, which also occurred in the 1930s, meant the removal of several Balby Road buildings. Much Council house building took place in the pre-war period too.

The scars of the war in Doncaster were particuarly felt in Balby's Western Road area where parachute mines caused widespread damage. A large number of houses were demolished or damaged and had to be evacuated.

In the post-war years, the decline in heavy engineering removed the brass works and wagon industry from Hexthorpe. The Plant Works has seen a drastic reduction in the workforce and in 1987 was split into three sectors, with one being run privately. However, Peglers' flourished, the factory expanding to cover many acres, with thousands of brass fittings being despatched each week from Balby to all parts of the world.

Hexthorpe house clearance began in the late 1950s, with the demolition of Bridge Terrace and Bridge Street. In subsequent years, and in spite of opposition, a road was cut through the allotments to join old Hexthorpe with Ramsden Road. Some building work also took place on the area.

In the same period, Balby Road, for some time the main western route for traffic from the town, underwent decline and decay. In 1961, the Balby Road Compulsory Purchase Order resulted in the forecourts and gardens of many Balby Road houses, shops and offices being sacrificed in a road widening scheme. The relatively new M18 motorway is now supposedly the main western thoroughfare out of the town, but Balby Road is as busy today as it ever was in the past. Balby, like Hexthorpe and many other outlying Doncaster areas, did not escape house clearance, including work being undertaken in the Queen Street, Stanley Street and Low Road areas.

This book includes pictures taken by several well-known photographers, amongst them are Luke Bagshaw, Edgar Leonard Scrivens, James Simonton and Geoff Warnes. I hope you have as much pleasure in looking at these as I had in choosing them.

Peter Tuffrey, April 1996

One
Rambling Round
the Area

Looking from the Cross Street/Oliver Road junction, Balby, towards Tickhill Road and Ashfield Road. On the left, the buildings include the Urban District Council Offices (formerly The Old Hall). Local photographer Luke Bagshaw was commisined to take the picture, illustrating the work to be carried out under the Doncaster Corporation Bill Session 1915 Street Widenings. Part of the site on the left is presently occupied by the Britannia Hotel, the license being transferred from East Laithe Gate/Silver Street corner, *c.* 1924.

View near the Balby Road/Carr Hill junction, looking towards the town centre, in the days when the Balby Road was devoid of motorised traffic. The road was very busy during Race Week. When the races were over, and folk were going home in wagonettes, many local kids congregated on Balby Road, shouting: 'hip, hip, hooray, throw your money away'. The racegoers throwing them threepenny bits and sixpences.

Taken in Balby Road, looking towards the town centre, the picture features the buildings (including the White Swan public house on the right), which were later demolished for the construction of Sandford Road.

Commercial property on the northern side of Hexthorpe Road, built *c.* 1900, and stretching between Denison Road and Kirk Street. The writing in the white-wash on two of the property's windows indicate they were subsequently occupied by A. Larner, cycle dealer and repairer, and J.S. Skinner & Co. hardware dealer.

Balby Road looking east, with Westfield Park on the left. Alice Fisher's trustees sold the park to the Doncaster Corporation during 1931, opening to the public during August the following year. The house within the area was demolished.

Hexthorpe Flatts was thrown open to the public on August Bank Holiday 1902, and has since become one of Doncaster's favourite parks. Shown here are swings and see-saws, built on the site of the old bandstand.

Balby Road, once part of the Tinsley and Doncaster Turnpike Trust, looking towards the Balby Bridge. At the time of the photograph *c.* 1910, properties on the right were largely for residential purposes, unlike today, having been converted for commercial use.

Another view of Balby Road facing the town centre. The tram track between Balby Bridge and the point here was single tracked with a passing loop at the Doncaster & District Steam Laundry Company's premises. The front gardens/forecourts of the properties on the right were mainly lost for road improvements under the Balby Road Compulsory Purchase Order, 1961.

Balby Road looking west, near the junction with Belmont Avenue. Many of these impressive houses were built during the latter half of the nineteenth century, and often occupied by professional people. Several properties in the centre of the picture have since been demolished, providing the site for the new Prince of Wales public house. This latter replaced the old Queen Street premises *c.* 1970.

King Edward Road, Balby, extending between Balby Road and Florence Avenue. Many of the properties were built in penny numbers during the Edwardian period, probably indicating how the thoroughfare acquired its name.

Dwellings on the southern side of Balby Road, stretching between Carr Hill and Carr View Avenue. Those extending from the small tobacconist's shop at the centre of the picture, up to and including Pillin's piano and organ warehouse, have since been demolished.

High Road, Balby, at the junction with Furnival Road, facing west. This picture was taken by local photographer Luke Bagshaw in connection with the Doncaster Corporation Bill Session 1915 Street Widenings. Properties on the left were lost during the late 1960s as part of the £400,000 phase of the Warmsworth Road dual carriageway scheme, extending between King Edward Road and Holly Terrace.

This picture is taken from the same position as the one above, but facing east. The Wesleyan Chapel on the right was demolished along with other properties for road improvements during the late 1960s. This latter work was carried out by Barnsley-based contractors John Hinchcliffe & Sons for a sum of £234,000.

Urban Road/Hexthorpe Road, Hexthorpe at the junction with Denison Road, looking towards Kirk Street. At the time the picture was taken *c.* 1905, this was the main thoroughfare through the area, carrying a section of the Hexthorpe tram route.

Urban Road, Hexthorpe at the junction with Chapel Street, facing the town centre. Littlewood Street is in the distance on the right. On the left, the property from which the lamp is attached is the Hexthorpe House, public house. These latter premises were rebuilt by Grimsby brewers Hewitt Bros in 1934. The road itself underwent much redevelopment during the early 1970s, as will be seen later in this book. The chapel closed in November 1958.

E.L.S. 1-222. Balby Road, Doncaster.

Two views of Balby Road taken, by local postcard view photographer Edgar Leonard Scrivens, in relatively peaceful times before the onslaught of motorised traffic. The properties look quite impressive too, a marked contrast to their present run down condition. Also, the rural feel has been lost as trees no longer overhang into the road from Westfield Park.

5 1-129. Balby Road, Doncaster.

St Catherine's Avenue, Balby, extending between Belmont Avenue and Carr Hill. The bulk of the properties were erected during the Edwardian period.

High Road, Balby near the junctions with Low Road and Green Field Lane. Car No. 12, purchased in 1903 was fitted with a top deck cover in 1913, and withdrawn from service in 1930. None of the properties on the right, extending from the tram to beyond the telegraph pole, exist today, having been cleared during the late 1960s for the Warmsworth Road dual carriageway scheme, stretching between King Edward Road and Holly Terrace.

The main house-building work in Shadyside, Hexthorpe, shown above, took place between the early 1890s and the outbreak of the First World War. A number of properties along the thoroughfare were demolished during the mid-1970s. The vicarage is out of view on the left.

Hexthorpe Road taken from near the junction with Flowitt Street, the latter having since been cleared. Note the cart in the foreground on the right, which seemingly belongs to the Elephant Hotel, St Sepulchre Gate, Doncaster. It also begs the question: What is it doing there?

Earlesmere Avenue, Balby extending between Florence Avenue and High Road. Plans for Earlesmere Avenue's construction were submitted in 1911.

Springwell Lane, Balby, at the junction with Finch Road, and looking towards Broomhouse Lane. The Springwell Lane properties were built from 1910 onwards.

Victoria Road, Balby looking towards Florence Avenue and, obviously, at the time of the picture, only the western side had been erected. The trees on the eastern side are overhanging from Westfield Park.

A view showing Low Road, Balby on the left, and High Road on the right. This view has been greatly altered since the completion of the Warmsworth Road dual carriageway scheme, stretching between King Edward Road and Holly Terrace. As well as 1,100 yards of dual carriageway, the scheme involved two pedestrian subways and ramps, and 350 yards of retaining wall at Low Road, which became a cul-de-sac.

Cross Street Balby, extending towards High Road/Warmsworth Road. Plans were submitted to erect the Cross Street properties in 1909.

Properties on Balby Road's southern side, the entire thoroughfare once being known as Balby's Town Moor Avenue. However, tramps were once frequently seen on Balby Road, knocking on doors trying to obtain some food, or making their way to and from the Workhouse on Springwell Lane.

This view of Low Road, Balby, extending between Corss Street and High Road, was taken facing the town centre. Low Road became a cul-de-sac around the late 1960s following the completion of the Warmsworth Road dual carriageway scheme.

Properties on the southern side of Warmsworth Road, Balby in the years following the extension of the Balby tram route in 1915 to Warmsworth. Plans to build houses along Warmsworth Road started to be submitted from around 1911.

Florence Avenue, Balby, stretching from Greenfield Lane to merge with Littlemoor Lane, is shown facing the town centre. The thoroughfare was formerly known as Fidler's Lane and plans to build houses along it started to appear from *c.* 1909.

Balby Road looking west with Westfield Park, also known as Fisher's Park, on the right. The entrance to the park was formerly adorned with massive ornamental gates. The photograph was taken when tall trees overhanging from the park into the main road did not interfere with traffic. It certainly would be a different story today.

Anelay Road, Balby.

Another tranquil view of Balby Road facing the town centre when the only traffic to be seen included a single decked tram and a man on horseback. A row of shops, becoming known as the 'Balby Market' was eventually built between the property on the right and Carr Hill. All the buildings seen on the right have since been cleared, Becky Jane's clothing factory occupying part of the site.

Brunswick Villas, built in 1907 on Balby Road's northern side. These properties, like many others on the thoroughfare had their front gardens, walls and railings removed to facilitate road improvements.

Low Road, Balby facing the town centre. At one time the thoroughfare contained a mortuary, the Boot & Shoe Inn, Shepherd's Yard and Shepherd's Row. Low Road was changed considerably following the Doncaster Balby Road/Warmsworth Road CPO, 1964. Tenby Gardens presently covers part of the site on the right.

This view, looking towards Furnivall Road, is seen from near the Balby High Road/Oswin Avenue junction. The Doncaster Corporation commissioned local photographer Luke Bagshaw to take the picture in connection with the Doncaster Corporation Bill Session 1915 Street Widenings.

This rather barren view shows the 'passing loop' near the junction of Warmsworth Road/Anelay Road, Balby. The Doncaster Corporation also commissioned local photographer Luke Bagshaw to take this picture in connection with the Doncaster Corporation Bill Session 1915 Street Widenings. Part of the site on the left is presently occupied by the Fairway Hotel, opened in 1929.

Balby Road with the Doncaster & District Steam Laundry Company's premises, opened in 1901, on the left. The manageress at this time *c.* 1910 was Miss Light.

The junction of High Road and Low Road, facing the town. Off centre to the left is the entrance to Greenfield Lane.

The Bandstand at Hexthorpe Flatts. During the summer months, band concerts were held on Monday and Thursday evenings 7 p.m. to 9 p.m., on Bank Holidays from 2 p.m. to 5.30 p.m. and in the evenings from 6.30 pm. to 9.30 p.m.

During the early Edwardian period, a Mrs H. Anderson, from Otley, obtained a contract to provide boats for hire along the River Don at Hexthorpe Flatts. The landing stage and an office is depicted here in these two photographs. A boat house built from limestone, by the Corporation, was erected in 1904. Following Mrs Anderson's death in 1905, her business venture was continued by family members.

Shops in Hexthorpe Road, extending between Kirk Street and Flowitt Street. Bill posters on H. Hemsworth's shop wall carry headlines from several newspapers including the *Daily Dispatch*, *Sheffield Independent*, and *Doncaster Chronicle*.

Hexthorpe Road, now Urban Road, Hexthorpe, looking towards the town centre. The Hexthorpe tram route was single tracked, containing only two passing loops. On the left is the entrance to Salisbury Road.

Furnivall Road, Balby, where plans to erect villas and cottages along the thoroughfare began to appear from around the early 1890s, most of the work being completed by the first decade of the present century. Builder and contractor John Furnivall, born at Tunbridge Wells, took a prominent part in the affairs of the district. He died aged 60 in 1903.

The Balby Road 'Market', extending at right angles from Carr Hill. Traders within the stretch of properties included Ben Ellis, E. Jowett, S. Boers, H. Craven, James Coombes & Co's boot repairing factory, H.A. Staton's hardware shop, F. Roberts' family butchers and H. Goddard's fish-and-chip shop.

Balby Road looking towards the town centre, with St John's church out of view to the left, and Low Road to the right.

Low Road, Balby, shortly before the area was redeveloped, and the houses, extending from the centre of the picture to the left, were demolished. Part of Scarborough Barracks may be seen on the right. This latter building was erected during 1951.

Balby Road facing the town centre. All the properties on the right, extending to Sandford Road, have since been demolished. The entrance, just off centre to the right, once led to Melville Avenue.

Warmsworth Road, Balby looking towards the tram terminus at Oswin Avenue. The picture was obviously taken before the route was extended to Warmsworth in 1915.

Cottages at the junction of Ashfield Road and Cross Street. The cottages, once numbered 30 and 32 Low Road, eventually became numbers 2 and 4 Ashfield Road. The latter property was demolished during September 1994.

Commercial premises on Hexthorpe Road, extending between Kirk Street and Flowitt Street, including those of fried fish dealer A.J. Swift, grocer and provision dealer Nettleship, and watchmaker and jeweller W. Senior. The view pre-dates the arrival of trams in 1902.

Cottages at the Ashfield Road/Cross Street corner. Only one property is extant today and its appearance is much altered from when the above photograph was taken.

The Primitive Methodist Chapel, Balby Road, built in 1868 at a cost of £740, which was not finally paid until 1912. Doncaster's first Primitive Methodist Society was established in 1820, services being held in Princes Street.

Tickhill Road looking towards Cross Street. The area on the right has since been occupied by the Britannia Hotel. The photograph was taken for Doncaster Corporation by local photographer Luke Bagshaw in connection with the Street Widenings Bill Session 1915.

Bowling at Hexthorpe Flatts, one of a number of activities still to be found in the area.

Oarsmen on the River Don around 1910. The boathouse may be clearly seen in the background. Boating was one of the main attractions of the pleasure grounds in Hexthorpe Flatts.

Houses under construction near the Shadyside/Laughton Road junction Hexthorpe, during July 1905, provide a backdrop for horse-drawn wagonettes conveying people to a picnic at Edlington. The outing may have been arranged in association, with the local St Jude's church, out of view to the right.

Taken from one of the high-rise flats, this bird's eye view shows many of Hexthorpe's features including the Nine Arch Bridge, the Hexthorpe Cold Stores, St James' church and schools, and the old workhouse. Note also the YMCA building in the foreground.

St James' Bridge station, near the Nine Arch Bridge, demolished during 1955.

Local transport photographer Geoff. Warnes captured AEC bus No. 22 passing Jubilee Clock Tower, Urban Road, Hexthorpe on 23 August 1969.

View along Littlemoor Street, Balby, demolished during the early 1970s.

Weston Road, Balby, off Sandford Road.

The Jubilee Clock Tower at the Shadyside/Urban Road junction. On the right is Denison
Road.

Two views of properties in Urban Road, Hexthorpe near the Mutual Street junction. The photographs were taken, looking towards the town centre, during the early 1970s, prior to the buildings being demolished for redevelopment.

Views of Stanley Street,
Balby, demolished
during the early 1970s.

View of Stanley Street, Balby, the bulk of which was built in penny numbers during the 1890s by a variety of builders including, Mullins & Richardson, T. Justice, Sprakes & Son, S. Beastall and A. Liversedge. The street was demolished in the early 1970s. Stanley Gardens now occupies part of the site.

Two

Businesses

Ernest Henry Booth's grocery, provisions and tobacco stores at 4 High Road, Balby. Whilst there are a number of commercial signs around the premises, the shop window is devoted to displaying soap advertisements by firms such as Sunlight, Brooke's, Lever's, Swan and Lux. Wording on Brooke's ad' reads 'Monkey Brand Won't Wash Clothes, Puts A Bright Face on Things'. The three wooden tubs on the right contain Armour & Co's Climax Pure Lard.

Sarah (left) and Elizabeth Gardom at their Tickhill Road home, 1926.

A group of Gardom &Whaley employees outside the laundry.

Outside the Gardom & Whaley business premises. John Whaley is on the right with the firm's horse-drawn cart.

Gardom & Whaley's Doncaster & Balby Laundry, opened during the late nineteenth century, operating from an old Girl's Reformatory, west of Balby Bridge and set back from the road. Surprisingly, the building survives today. The business was run by the Gardom sisters Elizabeth, Sarah, Maggie May and Grace, together with the latter's husband John William Whaley. Maggies's involvement however, seems to have ceased in 1899 following her marriage; Sarah and Elizabeth never married. The Doncaster & Balby Old Laundry competed with an adjacent firm called the Doncaster & District Steam Laundry Company Limited, opening in 1901. And, for the first quarter of the new century at least, they seemingly co-existed well enough together. The Doncaster & District Laundry Co. Ltd advertised extensively in local newspapers throughout this period, whereas Gardom & Whaley appeared to rely on word-of-mouth. The Gardom sisters and John Whaley were keen Methodists, being strongly connected with Balby's Primitive Methodist Church. John Whaley, over a period of time, held all the offices of the church including choir master and treasurer. Additionally, he worked as a member of the Manchester Unity of Oddfellows (Lord Milton Lodge) and was secretary for twenty-five years. He was also a life govenor of the Doncaster Infirmary. He and his wife had no children. Maggie was the only Gardom sister to produce a child, a girl who took her mother's name. In 1926, Gardom & Whaley decided to retire from the laundry business, as announced in a sale notice which appeared in the *Doncaster Gazette*, 21 January of that year. John Whaley only saw four years of his retirement. His wife died in 1945, Elizabeth in 1940, Sarah 1955 and Maggie (snr) 1959. The Doncaster & District Laundry Co. Ltd continued in existence until the building was demolished for redevelopment *c.* 1970, although as previously mentioned, Gardom & Whaley's premises are still extant at the rear of the Kwik-Fit Balby Road site.

A van belonging to the Doncaster & District Steam Laundary Co. Ltd, Balby Road.

A splendid view of one of Slack's wagons stacked with soda syphons and bottles. The location, however, is unidentified.

Henry Hemsworth's tobacconist and newsagent's shop at 30 Hexthorpe Road, Hexthorpe. When Henry's widow Elizabeth died in 1953 aged 91, she had been in business more than fifty years, and was the town's oldest newsagent.

Scene outside Frederick Pedley's Hexthorpe Dairy at 36 Hexthorpe Road.

Butcher George William Brammer's horse-and-cart is captured adjacent to the business premises at the Denison Road/Urban Road junction. George Brammer died in 1912.

An employee of the Doncaster & District Steam Laundry & Window Cleaning Company, poses for the camera outside the business premises opened in 1901 in Balby Road. The company was established to carry on the business of steam and general laundry proprietors, dyers, cleaners, carpet beaters, window cleaners etc. One of the company's advertisements in 1911 claimed that window cleaning was carried out by most competent and reliable men; carpet beating and cleaning by the latest vacuum process.

The frontage of Reg Elliff's Balby Road camera shop is depicted here. A tiny cinema contained within the premises is shown below. The cinema, operating during the 1930s, measured 24 ft by 6 ft, with six seats. Reg moved the photographic business to Cleveland Street during the 1950s, and Denaby a decade later, where it still thrives today, under his son Ken.

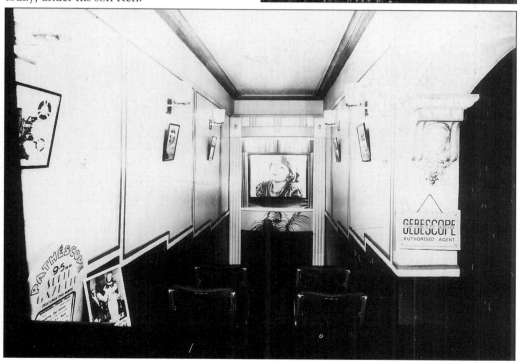

J.H. Hall & Son's The Park Motor Works, Balby Road, Balby. In 1931, the business was subsequently taken over by W. Scrimshaw & Son, and is still thriving under that family name today.

The Oak Garage Co.'s premises on High Road Balby, demolished for road widening during the 1960s. A former employee, Gordon Dexter continues the firm's name today in property along Earlesmere Avenue.

Uppadine's cycle shop at the Balby Road/Alexandra Road corner. The business closed during the early 1970s.

Three
Events

A crowd of residents poses for patriotic celebrations in the middle of Belmont Avenue, Balby. And, some remarkable expressions may be seen on faces young and old. The street links Balby Road and St Catherine's Avenue.

A set of three pictures, two on this page and another on the page opposite, depicting scenes of celebration, street parties and fancy dress parades, in Bridge Street Hexthorpe, 1945. The street was demolished during the 1950s.

Bridge Street celebrations, Hexthorpe.

Flags wave and the traffic stops as King George VI and Queen Elizabeth pass the Sandford Road/Balby Road junction, 11 Spetember 1948.

Two views showing members of the Balby Bridge Novelty Band in a fine array of fancy dress. The collection boxes in the photograph below bear the words Doncaster Infirmary, indicating the pictures were probably taken during the band's sterling efforts to raise funds for the institution. At the Comrades of the Great War Comic Band Contest they were presented with a special silver cup, the gift of an anonymous donor, in recognition of their services on behalf of the funds of the Doncaster Infirmary. A remarkable fact was that only two members of the band had any knowledge of music and that all their selections were played 'by ear'. The photograph above was taken outside the Balby Bridge Working Men's Club & Institute, Roberts Road.

Feast Day celebrations in Queen Street, Balby. The protruding lamp in the centre of the photograph belongs to the Prince of Wales public house. The street was demolished *c*. 1968.

A Band of Hope Demonstration passes along Low Road, Balby, at the junction with Grange Avenue, during August 1916.

Posing for the camera at Balby Feast. This event was frequently held in Westfield Park and later on an area off Sandford Road.

From a cart belonging to Slack's Mineral Water Co., the Revd Gore Rees says a few words to those attending an Infirmary Sunday Demonstration, at Balby.

E.L.S. 11. FIRE AT WOODHOUSE & CO'S BRASS WORKS, DONCASTER, Sep 22nd 1908.

Woodhouse & Co's Brass Works, Hexthorpe, started in 1873 in a former oil cloth factory, and was situated along Factory Lane, later called Foundry Road. Extensive damage, estimated at about £15,000, was caused by a fire on 23 September 1908, though the amount was covered by insurance. Four hundred men were thrown out of employment for a time and there was no clue to the cause of the outbreak.

Huge crowds gather round for the unveiling of the Great War Memorial at St Jude's Church, Hexthorpe during May 1921. Hexthorpe had 106 heroes who made the ultimate sacrifice during the Great War. The dedication of the memorial was performed by Archdeacon Sandford. St Jude's Church was erected in 1894, at a cost of £5,000, by Lord Grimethorpe and Miss Beckett-Dennison.

Scenes in Albany Road, Balby amidst the Victory in Europe celebrations. Plans were submitted to erect houses along this thoroughfare from around 1904.

E.L.S. I. DONCASTER TERRITORIALS LEAVING ST JUDE'S CHURCH JULY 18TH 1905

Two views taken by local photographer Edgar Leonard Scrivens of the Doncaster Territorials leaving St Jude's Church Hexthorpe 18 July 1902, and moving along Hexthorpe Road.

E.L.S. 2. DONCASTER TERRITORIALS LEAVING ST JUDE'S CHURCH, JULY 18TH,

Where are they now? The children pictured here making sure that the rather impressive Humpty Dumpty does not fall off the wall. They are part of a carnival parade, organised in association with the Plant's Carriage & Wagon Works' Sports Day, moving along Bridge Terrace, Hexthorpe. The thoroughfare, becoming known as Bridge Terrace, was originally titled Cherry or Love Lane. Most of the houses were built during the latter half of the nineteenth century. Eventually, there were thirty-nine Bridge Terrace properties. It is almost certain that the dwellings were intended to house workers at the Plant. Bridge Terrace and Bridge Street were cleared as a result of the Bridge Street Compulsory Purchase Order, 1958. Initially, the vacant area was scheduled to become an 'open space', but this was changed and it now forms a small industrial estate. A section of the Plant Hotel (dating from at least 1855, and rebuilt *c.* 1902) may be seen on the right.

Amidst Union Jack flags and bunting strewn across the street, a tea party is being staged by Balby's Regent Street residents as part of the town's contributions to the 1910-1935 Silver Jubilee celebrations. Regent Street extends between Low Road and Woodfield Road.

Left: A sheik with a camel is definitely not a spectacle familiar to people in Hexthorpe Road, Hexthorpe. But on this occasion they are pictured as part of a carnival parade, organised in association with the Plant's Carriage & Wagon Works' Sports Day. Right: Athough described as an 'uninvited guest', this dishevelled gentleman seems to have been provided with, and enjoying, a cuppa, a few cakes and biscuits at a tea party organised by Balby's Regent Street residents for the 1910-1935 Silver Jubilee celebrations.

During 8-9 May 1941, parachute mines were dropped among the Council houses (shown here) near the Weston Road hospital at Balby and at Ellers Road, Bessacarr. In these, eighteen were killed and thirty-two seriously injured. About twenty-five houses were destroyed and many others, including the Waverly School at Balby, were badly damaged. One of the mines fell harmlessly behind St Catherine's at Balby.

In 1947, eighteen people were killed in a train crash at Balby Bridge. Four years later, and very near to the same spot, fourteen people were killed in another railway crash, seen in the above photograph. The two accidents had nothing in common. It was pure coincidence and signalling was not at fault. The fourteen victims included a family of three. A further eighteen casualties were admitted to Doncaster Infirmary – five men, five women and two children being seriously hurt. The disaster occurred within a minute of the train, which was formed of two trains from Hull and York, leaving Doncaster station at 10.08 a.m. Wreckage was strewn over five sets of rails and it was not until 11 p.m. that the main lines south of the town were cleared for traffic.

The *Cock-o'-the- North* engine, rebuilt in Doncaster in 1943, and the first two of the fourteen coaches passed safely beneath the bridge. Coach number three left the rails and smashed into a brick buttress below the bridge. The force of the impact sheared the coach in half and folded it around the buttress – half in and half out of the tunnel. It was from the wreckage of this coach that ten bodies were recovered and most of the injured released. Behind it, the four following coaches were hurled from the line. Two were partially telescoped. Emergency workers were on the scene within three minutes of the smash. An ambulance arrived in seven minutes and great work was done by police, fire brigades and the public.

At the inquiry into the incident the most dramatic evidence came from a twenty-two year old signal department labourer Norman Peach, working near the entrance to Balby Bridge: 'I looked round to see if I was clear when I heard the train coming. The engine was passing me and I noticed the name *Cock-o'-the-North*. I saw sparks coming from the bogies of the third coach. Then I saw the coaches sway off the rail. I shouted to my mate and the next thing I knew all the coaches were coming for us. I jumped into an alcove and the coach smashed into the stonework of the bridge pier. The train seemed to be gathering speed it was puffing hard'.

A newsreel film of the crash, taken by a *Doncaster Chronicle* and *Evening Post* staff photographer, was screened at the Essoldo Cinema in Silver Street for a period and at other cinemas, showing Universal and Gaumont-British news, throughout the country.

Four
Buildings

John Thomas Bagshaw founded the firm of Bagshaw & Son in 1897, though the father involved himself solely with its administration, which he coupled with an already-established grocery business. Clearly, as son Luke is listed as a working photographer as early as 1894, then operating from his parent's home in Union Street, the setting up of the 1897 business was intended as a vehicle for Luke's growing professionalism supported by his father's business acumen. Seen here, though not very clearly, is Bagshaw & Son's St James' Bridge photographic studio, Hexthorpe, occupied 1897/8, before the subsequent move to 150-152 St Sepulchre Gate. Traders posing with their horses and carts seemingly provided Luke a regular income.

The Balby Cinema, High Road, Balby, was opened on 5 September 1921, by the Mayor of Doncaster, Councillor S. Morris. Designed by architect P.A. Hinchcliffe, the building's frontage was in artificial stone, pebble-dashed with sand rock arches. The cinema closed on 11 June 1960.

Ashmount, High Road, Balby, before conversion to a Working Men's Club. The club, founded in 1908, was affiliated in 1912.

Five
The Plant

View inside the Plant Works' New Erecting Shop, built by H. Arnold & Son Ltd, in 1890/1 at a cost of £13,000. The new building consisted of two large erecting bays and a smaller bay for machinery. Both erecting bays accommodated a centre road with pits on either side. Each pit was capable of holding five engines. Two 30 ton overhead cranes, supplied by Messrs Craven Bros Manchester, were housed in both of the erecting bays. The west side of the Shop (looking north) is shown here c. 1905.

The Crimpsall repair shop under construction in June 1899. The scheme began in that year after difficulties over the sale of the land were overcome. Construction work was carried out by local builders H. Arnold & Son Ltd at a cost of £294,000. The entire workshop could hold around 100 engines.

Interior of the Crimpsall repair shop *c.* 1905, looking west down 1A Bay.

During 1900 tender repair work in the Plant Works was moved to a new building (shown here under construction) at the west end of the Crimpsall repair shop. The new tender shop could hold thirty-two tenders.

In this c. 1905 view, looking eastwards down 1A Bay in the Crimpsall repair shop, bench fitting and turning work is being undertaken on motion gear, brakes and con rods.

This photograph shows locomotives undergoing repair in 1 Bay of the Crimpsall repair shop *c*. 1905. At this time, when working to capacity, the shop could repair 100 engines and sixteen tenders. The average time taken to carry out heavy repairs to a locomotive was about sixty working days. Workers operated in groups or gangs, under the supervision of a chargehand, and had six or seven engines in the course of dismantling or re-erecting at any one time. An engine, received in the Crimpsall repair shop for repair, was partially stripped on the centre road of a bay, lifted off its wheels and placed on an erecting pit, where stripping was completed. The various parts were transported, via trolley roads and electric tractors, to the boiling and cleaning tanks, and subsequently distributed to the various shops for repairs or replacement. The re-erection of the engine commenced when the repairable parts were dealt with and parts for replacement manufactured.

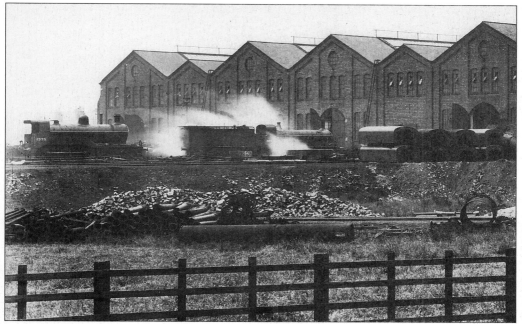

A general view of the Crimpsall repair shop, taken from the River Don on 21 July 1908, includes an Ivatt 4-4-0 No. 1375 and a Stirling 0-6-0 No. 365. It is possible that the Stirling engine is being 'steam' cleaned before entering the repair shop. Note also the pile of saddle tanks on the right.

These two engines belong to Patrick Stirling's 2-4-0 Class. H.A. Ivatt started to rebuild seventy-three of Stirling's engines in 1898, incorporating a 4 foot 5 inch diameter boiler and a flat-topped cab. No. 867 and the other locomotive behind it, whose number cannot be identified, display these new features. Both engines are pictured on the south side of the Crimpsall repair shop in June 1923 when No. 867 and several other 2-4-0s were withdrawn.

This is one of a group of photographs taken during November 1942 of women working in the Plant Works during the Second World War. The woman here is rivet heating in E. 1 Shop.

This is one of a set of pictures taken on 1 August 1945, showing Bruce Woodcock, the heavyweight boxing champion of Great Britain and the British Empire, working as a fitter in the Plant Works.

The first A2/3 No. 500 (later 60500) was named *Edward Thompson*, after its designer, and was the 2,000th engine to be built by the Plant. It is pictured there shortly after completion during the 1940s.

Standard Class 4, 2-6-0 locomotive No. 76114, one of 115 of that type, was the last steam engine to be built at Doncaster. It is seen here with a number of the Plant staff on 14 October 1957.

Six
Peglers

Austin Turnbull pictured in Peglers' Toolroom during 1963, when he was the firm's longest serving employee (fifty-two years).

Frank Pegler,
Chairman 1899 - 1938.

F. Birchall,
Managing Director 1899 - 1938,
Chairman 1938 - 1947.

Frank Pegler and Fred Birchall set up a brass foundry in Union Street, Doncaster during 1899, production starting a year later with around seventy employees. The foundry mainly manufactured products for the steam industry. By 1903, the company had a debt of £3,600 and there was a need to move to larger premises, increasing production to make a profit. In 1904, land was purchased at Balby, and Belmont Works was built. With the outbreak of the First World War, the company produced shell fuses and sockets. The factory also made a Sopwith Cuckoo aircraft. After the cessation of hostilities, the factory resumed manufacturing water fittings, steam and radiator valves. Chromium plating was also introduced. In the Second World War, Peglers' produced shells, fuses, taps and valves for military use. *Ark Royal* was fitted with 6,000 Pegler non-concussive taps. There were sub-contracts for Rolls-Royce, Vickers Armstrong and British Thermostat with over 2,000 Pegler employees engaged in the War effort.

Peacetime production was very much geared to the housing programme, while Fred Birchall retired at the age of 77 in 1947. In 1955, a controlling interest was acquired in the Canadian Galt Brass of Ontario and to keep pace with the introduction of new materials, Paragon Plastics was formed in 1957, manufacturing plastic pipes, tubing and specialised products.

The first orders for small bore radiator valves were received in 1962 and the firm became known world-wide for these products, selling to more than 100 countries. The Pegler home base was firmly secured with service depots in Glasgow, London, Manchester, Salisbury, Washington, Bury St Edmunds and Birmingham. During 1968, Pegler (Holdings) Ltd, as the company and its subsidiaries were known, merged with Hattersley Holdings, until being taken over by F.H. Tomkins. Pegler Ltd now have one of the most modern factories of its type in Europe. To the customer, this means a base for a continuous, superior standard of production.

Product innovation has been the keynote of the company marketing and sales programme in the past few years, including the launch of the new kitchen and bathroom taps and handles, which are designer-based; the introduction of showers, the acquisition and extension of the renowned Sunvic range of domestic hot water and central heating controls and system packs. Together with an extensive range of other plumbing and heating products, these have kept Peglers' in line with changing laws, times and demands.

Peglers' general office in 1922 – in the foreground B. Trethewey and W. Wicks.

Peglers' rough stores.

Finishing shop.

Old machine shop.

Jim Douglas in the foundry, spring 1963.

Peglers' staff about 1930.

Exhibition stand showing Peglers' products.

The extruding plant about 1962.

D. Atkin and C. Smart in the Automatic Plating Plant, spring 1963.

Screwdown assembly group, spring 1963. From left to right: P. Gleadall, L. Soar, M. Savage, F. Fabrik, B. Scott, J. Walker, N. Halkier, R. Potts, M. Jackson, J. Marshall, B. Marriot, E. Smith, C. Hunt, R. Hall, N. Whinfrey, G. Waite, H. Cooper, J. Walters.

Employees at work on the Flow Line Inspection, spring 1963.

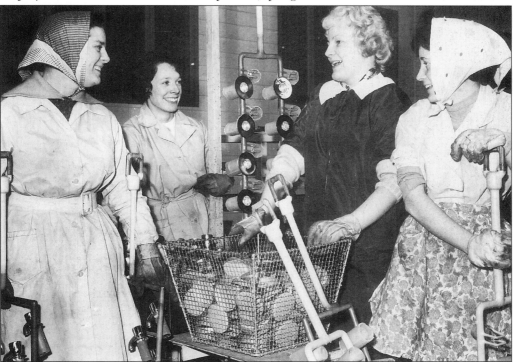

Jigging and Auto Plating Shop Group, Spring 1963. From left to right: C. Lacey, C. Smith, M. Walshaw, B. Booth.

Mayor of Doncaster, Councillor Gerry McDade visits the Works in 1976.

Mrs P. Wilson operating M/C in the Girl's Machine Shop. Looking on are M. Stenson and W. Cooper (foreman), during spring 1963.

Aerial view of works c. 1968.

T. Piper M/C operator Die-Casting Department. Looking on are Staff Setter S.F. Rowlands and R. Harper, during spring 1963.

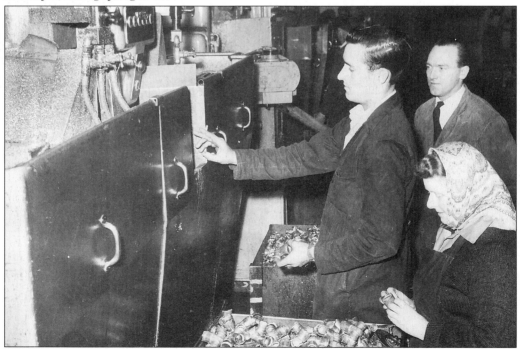

Diedesham Tapping Machine N.B. Automatic Department, (A. Harper supervising), spring 1963.

Seven

Trams and Trolleybuses

With simple tools and equipment, labourers lower a 'centre grooved' rail into position to establish a passing loop at the corner of Spansyke Street in Hexthorpe. Although Doncaster and Hull were the only tramway systems to employ 'centre grooved' rails in the electric era, the Liverpool horse tramways and Dudley-Wolverhampton steam tramways had utilised a similar type of rail in the 1880s and 1890s.

Car 19 was photographed, in pristine condition, at the Hexthorpe 'outer' terminus in Bramworth Road. Many of the old buildings in this area have since been demolished. Most people used the Hexthorpe tram service when travelling to Hexthorpe Flatts, a popular recreation area, and only a short distance from Bramworth Road. The Hexthorpe tram route was converted to trolleybus operation in 1929.

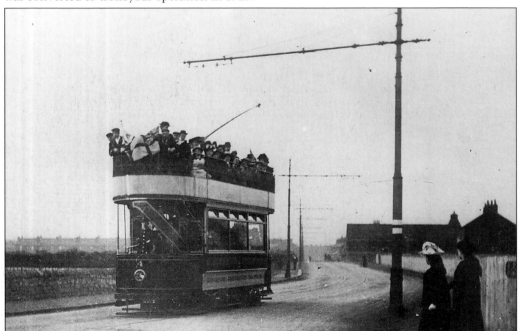

This photograph may have been taken on the opening day of the Hexthorpe route, 2 June 1902, since 'normal' service cars rarely carried as many passengers as those depicted here. Car 4 is seen in Urban Road prior to terminating in 'old' Hexthorpe; Greenfield Lane is on the right.

A view taken during the First World War of Car 19, in a very battered condition, at the junction of Urban and Bramworth Road. Female staff were not employed until the First World War when they replaced men that had enlisted in the forces. Four conductresses began work in July 1915, qualifying during the following Spring as tram drivers. Gradually, most cars were operated by female crews maintaining the tramway service for the duration of the war.

The Hexthorpe tram service was mainly used by workers from the Plant Works, Co-operative Stores, Burnett's Wagon Works and Woodhouse's Brass Works, with many fewer passengers at other times of the day. Car No. 19 is pictured at the Hexthorpe terminus in Bramworth Road.

Car 16 was photographed at the terminus in 'old' Hexthorpe. The open top-deck of a tram was certainly pleasant to travel on during the fine weather but when it was wet or cold, passengers tended to congregate on the lower deck. As the Board of Trade stipulated trams could only carry eight standing passengers, their passenger load was seriously reduced during inclement weather and was the main reason that most of Doncaster's cars were fitted with 'top-deck' covers by 1913.

Car 15 at the terminus in 'old' Hexthorpe.

The original Balby tram terminus pictured here in these two photographs was at the junction of High Road/Oswin Avenue. The tracks ended in a 'Y' arrangement (a characteristic feature of Doncaster tramways) on either side of the tram shelter. This building had to be locked at certain times to restrict vandalism and was eventually moved. On 4 February 1915, the Balby route was extended to Warmsworth.

When women began their duties with the Tramways' Dept no-one knew whether to call them, 'motoress', 'motorwoman', or 'driver'. In this photograph the female crew of Car No. 27 take a rest from their duties and pose for the camera at Oswin Avenue, in 1917.

Car No. 6, purchased in 1902, fitted with a top-deck cover in 1913 and withdrawn in 1930, is pictured on a Beckett Road/Balby cross-town service.

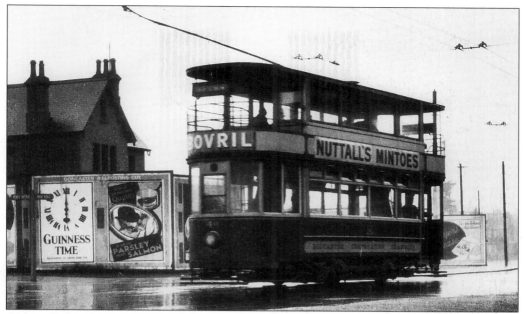

Although the tram terminus at Balby was abandoned in 1915, a service continued to operate to Balby, mainly at busy times. On the last day of tram operation on the route, Car No. 46 is photographed leaving Oswin Avenue, carrying only a few passengers.

Cars numbered 40 and 42 are seen together on a 'passing loop' at Oswin Avenue, Balby on the last day of tram operation on the route, 25 July 1931. Car No. 40 was the last tram to run in Doncaster on 8 June, 1935.

Trolleybuses 27 and 28 pass one another near Oswin Avenue, Balby, on the first day of trolleybus operation on the Balby route, 26 July 1931. The Balby route became the busiest trolleybus service. Six vehicles usually operated on the route during weekdays with ten on Saturdays. Trolleybus crews often complained that twelve minutes allowed for the outward journey and thirteen for the return was impracticable, since the route was very busy and there were sixteen stops to make.

Trolleybus No. 18, in service between 1930 and 1938, is seen working on the Hexthorpe route.

Trolleybus No. 365, stranded in Urban Road, near the Hexthorpe Jubilee Clock, on 9 April 1955.

Trolleybus No. 353 passing the junction of Urban Road/Scarll Road. The vehicle was in service between 1 March 1958 and 28 March 1963. The chassis of Nos 353 and 354 were purchased second hand from the Mexborough & Swindon Traction Co.

Trolleybus No. 374, passing along Bridge Terrace, Hexthorpe during the 1950s.

Trolleybus No. 365 displaying the Balby route number 10, passes the Steam Laundry in Balby Road, 24 September 1955.

A Balby trolleybus passing the 'Balby Market' buildings during the 1950s. Note how the traffic has built up since the days when trams operated along the thoroughfare, illustrated earlier in the book.

View of a trolleybus passing along Bridge Terrace, Hexthorpe, after the area, along with Bridge Street, had been cleared during the late 1950s.

Trolleybus No. 374 is pictured with both the conductor and driver at the Hexthorpe outer terminus on 7 August 1954. Trolleybus crews had to adhere to a strict time schedule on the Hexthorpe route. The outward and return journeys were only supposed to take ten minutes and there were quite a number of stops to make.

Karrier 'E6' trolleybus, fleet No. 367, moves along Balby Road past Burton Avenue on 19 September 1954. During August and September 1957, this vehicle and No. 368 were the last three-axle trolleys to operate in Doncaster.

Trolley No. 357 gliding along Balby Road on 24 September 1955.

The driver and conductor of Karrier 'E6' D/D trolleybus No. 351 pose for the camera at Barrel Lane. Sometimes during the autumn months the trolleybus crews, with the aid of a 'trolley pole', would help the local youngsters to obtain 'conkers' from a Horse Chestnut tree nearby.

Trolleybus No. 374 is seen leaving Bridge Terrace, Hexthorpe, before crossing St James' Bridge, on its way back to the town centre.

Eight
Licensed Premises

The Prince of Wales public house, Queen Street, Balby *c.* 1914. The premises were occupied for some time by the Pickering family.

The White Swan, Balby Road shortly before demolition *c.* 1934, the site being required to facilitate the construction of Sandford Road. New premises were erected on the opposite side of Balby Road.

The Vine Hotel, Kelham Street Balby, *c.* 1906 was licensed in 1890, another inn of the same name having existed in Balby until 1851. At the time of the picture, Thomas Avill was the licensee.

Sunnyside Beer Off 11 Shadyside, Hexthorpe, run by George Prime at the time the photograph was taken c. 1970.

Regulars pictured outside the Prince of Wales, Queen Street, Balby, which was demolished c. 1969. New premises were subsequently opened in Balby Road.

The Prince of Wales, Queen Street, Balby pictured during the clearance of the thoroughfare on 4 February 1969.

Pickering's Brewery, Back Lane, Balby pictured *c*. 1910. The business, operating during the first few years of the present century, was run by Frank Pickering.

Two photographs showing the old and new Plough Inn, High Road, Balby. The old premises, dating from at least 1822, were rebuilt in 1904. Grimsby-based brewers, Hewitt Bros, were once owners of the pub.

Hexthorpe House, Urban Road, Hexthorpe, dating from at least 1871, being rebuilt in 1934.

The Prior Well Inn, situated at the Littlewood Street/Urban Road corner, Hexthorpe. The premises dated from at least 1877 and were once owned by Joseph Garside, and the Worksop & Retford Brewery Co. Ltd.

The Rising Sun public house, at the junction of Flowitt Street/Hexthorpe Road, Hexthorpe, dating from at least 1839, the premises being enlarged around 1896. Quite a number of clubs once met at the pub, including the Rising Sun Anglers Association, which had a membership of seventy.

The Prior Well Inn shortly before demolition *c.* 1974. The inn was formerly the headquarters of the Balby-with-Hexthorpe Allotment Gardeners' Society.

The Boot & Shoe public house, Low Road Balby, dating from at least 1864. At the time the photograph was taken c. 1905, W. Sharpe was the licensee. The premises closed in 1924.

Nine
Formal Groups

Plant Works football team 1918-19.

Balby School, 1913. The picture was taken by local photographers, J. Simonton & Son.

Balby Cricket Club, 1920s.

Hexthorpe Primitive Methodist C.C. Champions Doncaster Non-conformist League 1907.

Tennis players at Eden Grove, Hexthorpe.

Peglers' Mens M/C shop group 1963. Back row, from left to right: D. Shepherd, J. Bostock, G. Frost and F. Parker. Remainder, from left to right: A. Blythe, P. Sutton, C. Poulton, D. Bramall, R. Barton, J. Dixon, G. Deakin, R. Bratley, E. Hall, C. Edwards.

Ten
Aerial Views

Aerial view taken 25 June 1951, from above the Doncaster Union Workhouse, looking towards the town centre.

Aerial view taken 25 June 1951, looking towards the town centre, with the White Church on the left.

Aerial view taken 25 June 1951, looking towards the town centre, with Westfield Park just off centre to the left.

Aerial view taken 25 June 1951, looking towards the town centre, with the Windsor Cinema off centre to the left.

Eleven
Redevelopment

The Springwell Lane workhouse and hospital, Balby was opened in 1900 and is seen here being demolished in 1974.

View from the Nine Arch Bridge, Hexthorpe, on 2 April 1955, showing St James' Bridge Station, being dismantled. A large proportion of Doncaster's September race traffic was handled by the station. Race days were usually Tuesday, Thursday and Friday; the St Leger being staged on Wednesdays. St James' Bridge Station was set in the fork of the old Great Northern and Great Central Railway Companies' routes, south-west of Doncaster. The building, though not in use for much of the year, boasted a complete set of signs, signals and an impressive 'hill-and-dale' roof.

Demolition men having a cuppa whilst clearing the Springwell Lane Workhouse and Hospital, Balby in 1974.

Before house clearance began in Hexthorpe during the early 1970s, much anxiety was expressed by residents, particularly the older ones, over whether they would be satisfactorily re-housed. They grouped themselves together forming the Hexthorpe Tenants' and Owners' Association and even wrote to Prime Minister Harold Wilson asking him to intervene. In the event, most were successfully accommodated. The photographs on this page show clearance work along Urban Road, where about 100 properties were demolished.

Work on the Balby Bridge interchange.

For many years the junction of Balby Road, St Sepulchre Gate and Green Dyke Lane experienced crippling traffic congestion – particularly at rush hours. During 1969, the old Doncaster Corporation commissioned Sheffield consultant engineers Husband & Company, to investigate the problem. The following year, the firm recommended a solution and in 1974, South Yorkshire County Council (who inherited the scheme under local government re-organisation) invited tenders. The contract – for £1,046,000 – was won by the Retford-based contractors A.F. Budge Ltd. The interchange project used 7,250 cubic metres of concrete, and 500 tons of reinforcement steel. Some 24,000 cubic metres of earth and rock were excavated. The interchange formal opening was during the summer of 1976, two months ahead of the official eighty week schedule.

Work on the Balby Bridge interchange.

Clearance work along Urban Road, *c.* 1974.

Urban Road, Hexthorpe, looking towards the town centre *c.* 1974, where clearance work is taking place near the Hexthorpe House pub.

The Prior Well Inn public house at the Littlewood Street/Urban Road junction, shortly before demolition in 1974.

G.M. Oliver's grocery and provision store in Urban Road Hexthorpe prior to demolition.

The original Doncaster & District Steam Laundry Co., Ltd's building in Balby Road, undergoing demolition. The Company was formed in 1901 and an advertisement once stated that 'high class laundry work of every description' was undertaken. A considerable amount was carried out for local schools, hospitals and hotels. Part of the site is now occupied by the Kwik-Fit, Tyre, Exhaust and Brake Centre.

The Old Doncaster Union Workhouse, built in Hexthorpe Road during 1840, undergoing demolition *c*. 1968. The work is being carried out by local firm Middleton's.